Contents

Section 1 — Investigating the Local Area 1

Section 2 — Improving the Environment 9

Section 3 — Village Settlers 15

Section 4 — A Village in Kenya 20

Section 5 — What's in the News? 27

Section 6 — Connecting to the World 32

Section 7 — How Do We Spend Our Time? 36

The Answers 41

Published by Coordination Group Publications Ltd.
Written by
Chris Parker
Eileen Worthington

Typesetting, Design and Graphics by
Martin Chester, Sandy Gardner, Sharon Keeley,
Simon Little, Becky May and Rachel Selway.
With thanks to Glenn Rogers *and* Barbara Melbourne *for the Proofreading.*

Maps reproduced from Ordnance Survey mapping by permission of the Ordnance Survey on behalf of the Controller of Her Majesty's Stationary Office, © Crown copyright, License No. 100034841.

ISBN 1 84146 750 2
Groovy Website — www.cgpbooks.co.uk

Printed by Elanders Hindson, Newcastle upon Tyne.
Jolly bits of clipart from CorelDRAW.
Text, design, layout and original illustrations © Coordination Group Publications Ltd. 2003
All rights reserved.

Section 1 — Investigating the Local Area

Finding the Local Area

Maps show places as if they have been drawn from above.
They are very useful for finding where places are.

1 Look at the world map below. Find the United Kingdom (UK) and (circle) it.

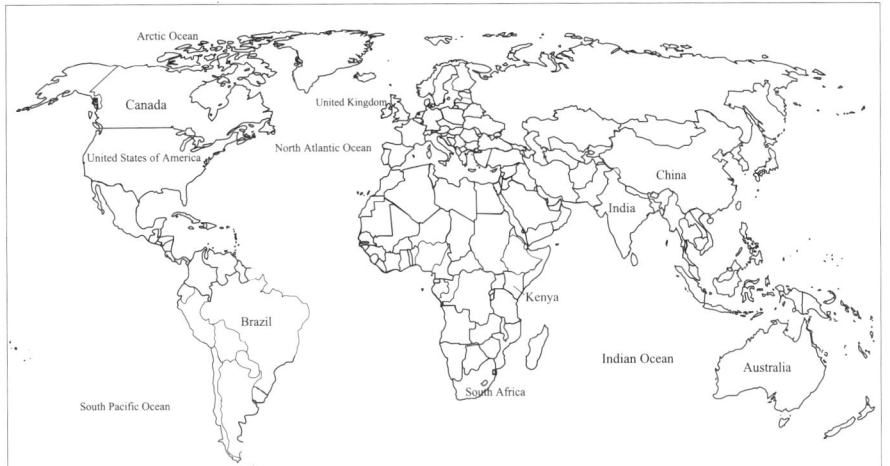

2 Tom lives in Essex in the UK (see the map below).
Complete the sentences using the words in the box.

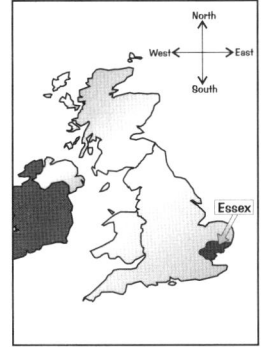

| counties | country |
| south-east | |

Tom lives in the .... called the UK.
The UK is divided into smaller areas, like Essex, called ....
Essex is in the .... of the UK.

A map of Tom's village is shown to the right.

3 Are these statements true or false?
Put a tick or cross in each box.

a) The school is south of the river. ☐
b) The village shop is on the north side of the High Street. ☐
c) Tom's house is on the west side of North Street. ☐
d) To get to The Fox pub from Tom's house, you go south down North Street, along The Green and turn left across the bridge into Fox Road. ☐

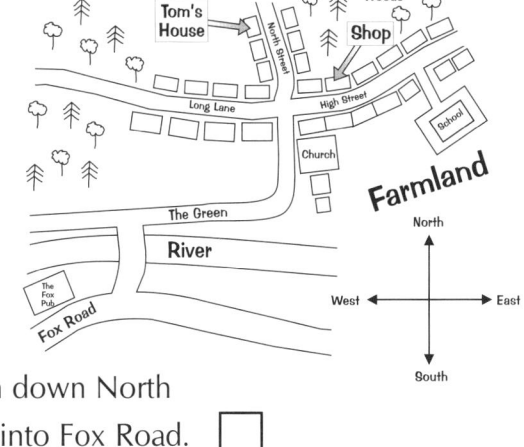

ACTIVITY *Different maps have different SCALES. This lets us see things in more or less detail. Find some different maps — a map of your <u>area</u>, of a <u>country</u> and a map of <u>the world</u>. Compare the scales of each map. How far is 1 cm on each map?*

Section 1 — Investigating the Local Area

Features You Can See in Villages

Villages are made up of human features (things that PEOPLE put there) and physical features (things that are NATURAL).

1 Look at the photo. The buildings are human features. Filling in the missing letters below to name three buildings in the picture.

a) a p....b

b) a h....us....

c) a ch....r....h

2 Below is a list of some other human land uses. Circle the 2 that you can see in the photo in Q1.

'Land use' is a geography phrase — it just means 'what the land is used for'.

playground   supermarket   road   factory   bridge

3 Here is a picture of the same village. The letters A to D mark physical (natural) features you can see. Complete the sentences below.

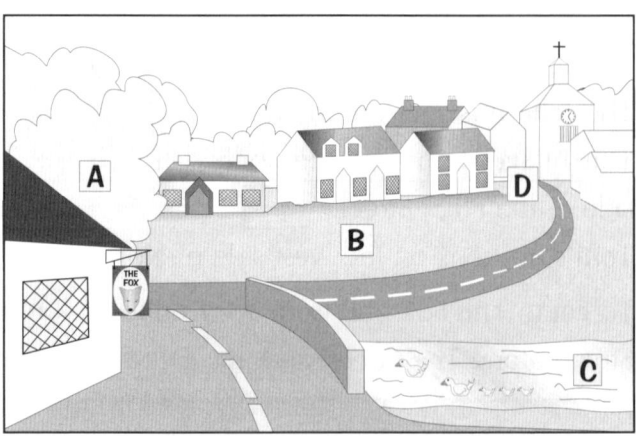

At **A**, you can see lots of t.....................
In front of the houses (at **B**) is the village g.....................
The village has been built near **C**, which is a r.....................
The church was built at **D**, on top of a small h.....................

Long ago this area was just a little hill by a river — now it's used for all sorts of things.

Section 1 — Investigating the Local Area

Layout of a Village

There are different land uses (like houses and shops) in different parts of the village.
The tricky bit is working out why the village layout is like this.

1 | Here is a map of the village Bottwiggle.

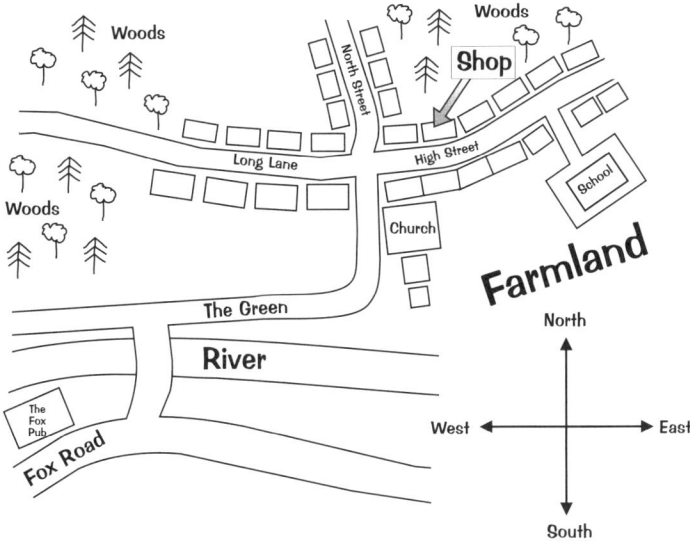

On the map:

a) **Draw a red line** around the buildings in the village centre. This marks the 'built-up area'.

Draw a red line around the pub.

b) **Colour** the woods green.

c) **Colour** the farmland brown.

2 | Look at where the buildings are on the map. Draw lines to match up the <u>buildings</u> listed below with the <u>reason they were built there</u>.

The pub	on the edge of the village where there is plenty of space.
The houses	in the centre of the village.
The church	on the main street where lots of people go.
The school	built close together around the church and the crossroads.
The shop	built as a place to stay where travellers had to cross the river.

3 | Use the words in the box to complete the sentences about the village layout.

| soils | attractive | flood |

There are no houses near the river because it might .... Trees have been planted to the west of the village to make the environment more ....
The land around the school has lots of farms because the .... are very fertile.

A village isn't just a jumbled-up collection of buildings. Everything is where it is for a reason.

Section 1 — Investigating the Local Area

Local Land Uses

A class from Bottwiggle school went to find out what land uses there were around High Street. The map shows what they found.

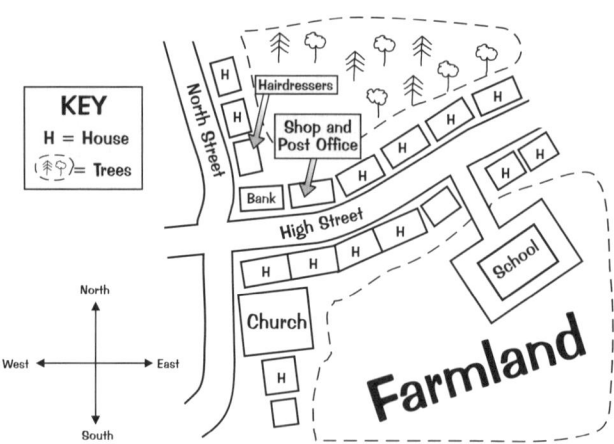

1 Colour in the different groups of land use on the map. The colours to use are in the colour key below. You should also colour each box to match.

COLOUR KEY

- [ ] Red for houses
- [ ] Yellow for services (buildings that people use, but not shops — e.g. school)
- [ ] Blue for shops
- [ ] Green for woodland
- [ ] Brown for farmland
- [ ] Black for roads

2 Look at the map in Q1, then fill in the table below by writing down the answers to the questions:

How many houses are there?	
How many services are there?	
How many shops are there?	

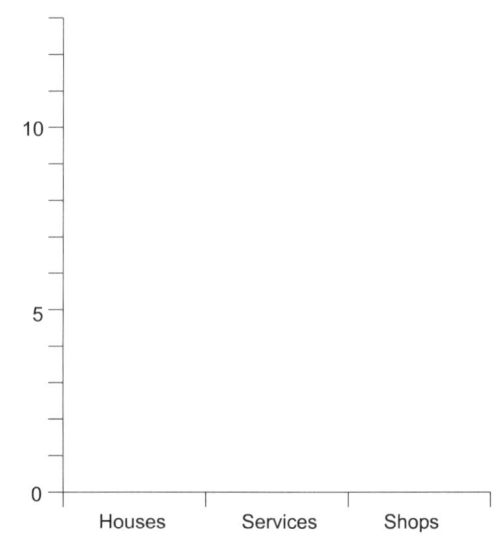

3 Show these numbers of buildings by drawing them on this bar chart:

Keys show us what all the different things on maps are — so we can find out even more.

Section 1 — Investigating the Local Area

Local Services

Bottwiggle village is small and doesn't have all the things that people need.
Many village people have to go to towns and cities to work and to go shopping.

1 Below is a list of some of the villagers' jobs. Look at the map on page 4 and circle the 4 jobs that can be done in the village.

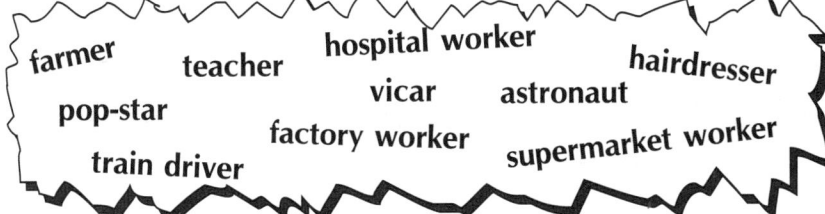

farmer, teacher, hospital worker, hairdresser, pop-star, vicar, astronaut, factory worker, supermarket worker, train driver

2 The map below shows the village and its surrounding area.

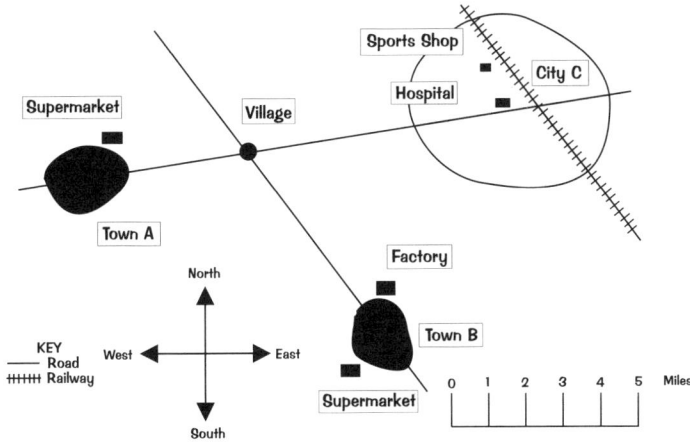

Circle the correct answer.

a) Where does the train driver go to work? to town A / to town B / to city C
b) Where does the factory worker go to work? to town A / to town B / to city C
c) Where does the hospital worker go to work? to town A / to town B / to city C
d) Where is the closest supermarket to the village? town A / town B / city C

3 Mr Patel lives in the village. Where does he have to go to do each thing below?

a) Buy a stamp to post a letter ...*the village*...

Is it the **village**, **town** or **city**?

b) Buy new trainers ....

c) Have his hair cut ....

d) Go for his hospital appointment ....

e) Do weekly supermarket shopping ....

Villages are small — so people often have to travel to other places for things they need.

Section 1 — Investigating the Local Area

How Villages Change

As time goes by, things in a village change — for example, people build new roads or houses.

1 A new road has been built on the edge of the village. Copy out 3 reasons why it was built from this list:

a) Too many big lorries drove right through the village.
b) The builders were bored and wanted something to do.
c) The village streets are too old and narrow.
d) People wanted to get to other places more quickly.

1 ....
2 ....
3 ....

2 Here is a photo of the new road. Circle the correct words below to show how the area's **ENVIRONMENT** has changed.

a) There is lots of **GRASS / TARMAC** where there used to be **GRASS / TARMAC**.
b) The old road through the village is **NOISIER / QUIETER** now.
c) The air round the new road is **CLEANER / DIRTIER** now.
d) **FEWER / MORE** wild animals live near the new road now.

3 Since the road was built, the environment inside the village has improved. Finish Suki's e-mail using these words:

| pollution | safer | quiet | lorries |
| traffic | fresh | dangerous |

Hi. Our village is so .... now that there is less ....
Very few big .... come through here now. My walk to school is much
.... It used to be very .... to cross the road. My mum says the
air smells .... because there is less ....

ACTIVITY Changes in the local area can seem good to <u>some people</u>, but bad to <u>others</u>. Imagine you are someone who is very unhappy about the new road. Write a letter to the Local Council explaining the problems it will cause.

Section 1 — Investigating the Local Area

Investigating Local Features

Old Mrs Morris is looking out of her window. She has lived in her house for over 50 years. and can remember when her view looked very different from what she sees today.

1 Below is a picture showing Mrs Morris's view today. Choose words from the box to label the human features (things that people put there). Write the correct words in the boxes A, B and C.

road   factory
housing estate

2 Sam wants to find out more about these features. Complete the missing words in his list of what he could do.

a) I could c............t how many houses there are.
b) I could draw a p.....ct........e of one of the houses.
c) I could take a ph.................... of the factory.
d) I could find out what the f.................y makes.

3 In the boxes below, draw pictures of these physical features (natural things) that can't be seen from Mrs Morris's window.

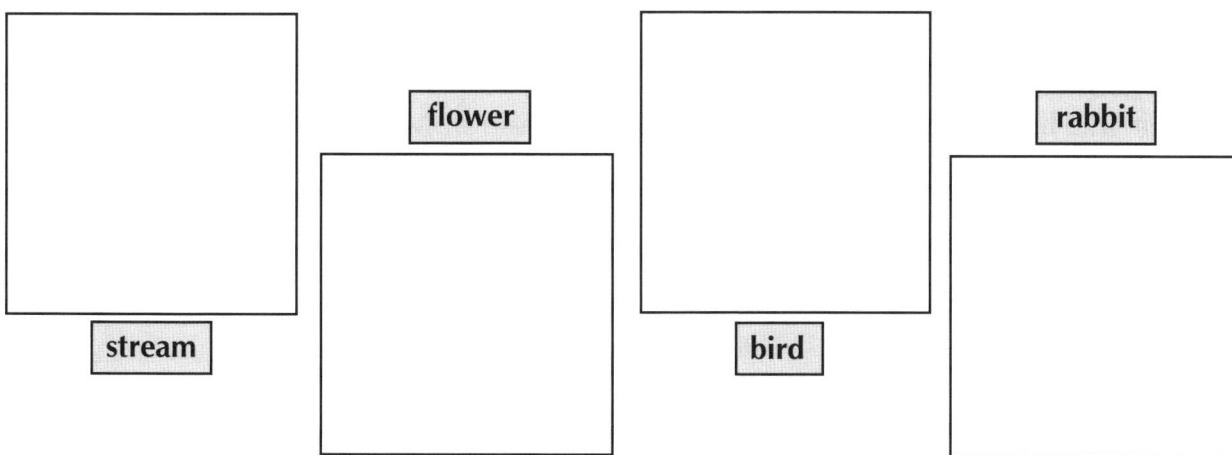

Try taking a photo or drawing a picture of the view that you can see from your window.

How Landscapes Change

Below is Mrs Morris's drawing of the view she saw through the same window over 50 years ago. You can see that it is different from the view on page 7.

1 Look at the picture. Use the words in the box to fill in the gaps in the sentences below.

| wood | houses |
| animals | narrow |

There is a .... on the right of the picture.
There are a few .... in the distance.
In front of Mrs Morris's house is a field of farm ....
The road is quite ....

2 Now look at the picture on page 7 as well as this picture. For each sentence below, write whether it's true TODAY or was true 50 YEARS AGO.

a) There is a large wood. ....
b) There is a factory. ....
c) There is a large housing estate. ....
d) There are fields of animals. ....
e) The road is very wide. ....

3 Changing the features in an area will normally lead to other changes too. Circle the things you think might have happened in Mrs Morris's view.

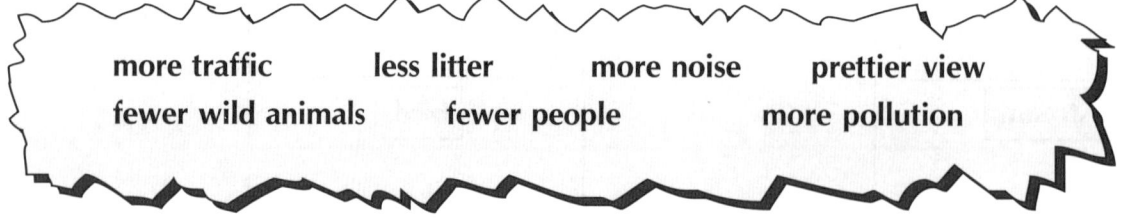

more traffic   less litter   more noise   prettier view
fewer wild animals   fewer people   more pollution

Changes like these happen all over the place. They usually make views less pretty to look at.

Section 1 — Investigating the Local Area

Section 2 — Improving the Environment

The School Environment

Lots of people spend time in schools every day — for example teachers, children, cooks, cleaners. Having so many people in one place at a time can cause environmental problems.

1 Match up the school activities below with the problems that they might cause.

ACTIVITY	ENVIRONMENTAL PROBLEM
Playing football on the playing field	Blocked roads and traffic jams
Parked cars waiting to collect children	Litter on the ground
Eating packed lunches and snacks	Trampled, muddy grass

2 There are different kinds of pollution. For each picture below, write underneath whether it is showing WATER pollution, AIR pollution or NOISE pollution.

a)

....

b)

....

c)

....

d)

....

3 The sentences below are about types of pollution. Use the words from the box to fill in the blanks.

Cars and .... arriving at school might cause AIR pollution.

.... might cause NOISE pollution for ....

School .... might cause WATER pollution if they flow into a ....

| stream | buses | playtime | neighbours | drains |

Pollution isn't the only environmental problem — things like litter and traffic can be a problem too...

Noise Pollution in Schools

Schools are noisy places — noise pollution is often a big environmental problem in schools. Different places in schools may be noisier at different times of day.

1 Look at the plan of a school below. Use words from the box to label the plan, showing what noise you would hear at each place in the school.

| singing   cars   clinking knives and forks   talking   shouting |

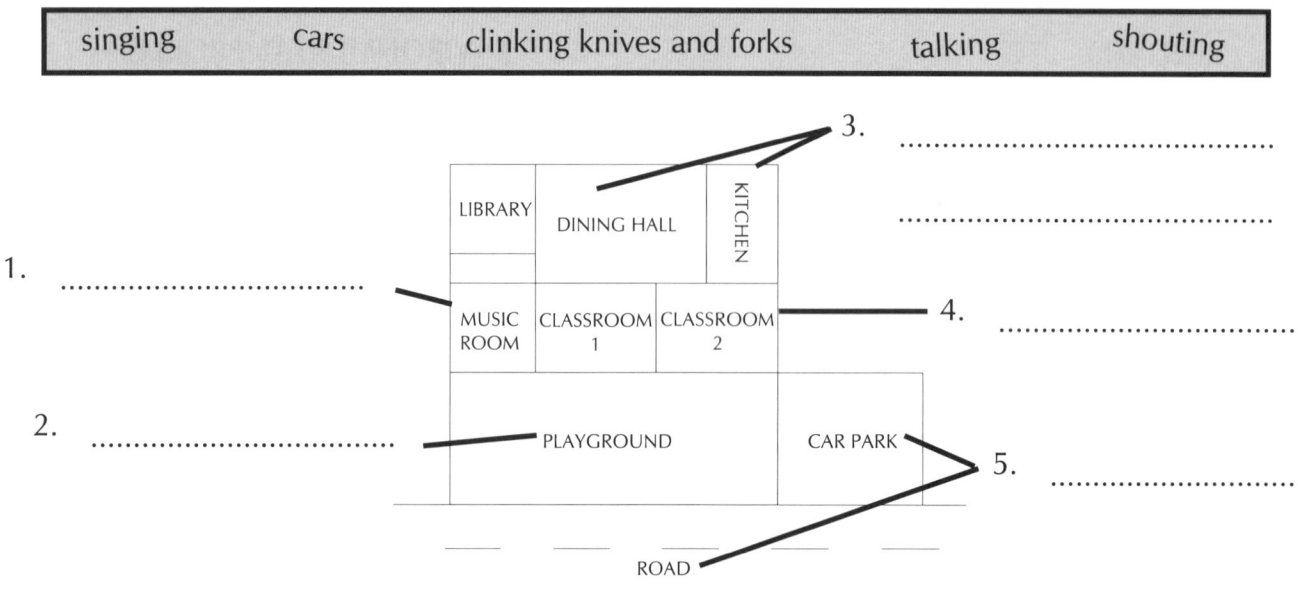

2 Some school areas are noisier than others because of what they're used for. Draw lines to match up each <u>school area</u> with its correct <u>use</u>.

School area
1. Classroom
2. Dining Hall
3. Library
4. Playground

Use
eating
quiet reading
playing
working

3 Look at the four school areas in Question 2. Write them in the boxes in order of how noisy each one usually is.

VERY NOISY ⟶ QUITE NOISY ⟶ QUITE QUIET ⟶ VERY QUIET

<u>ACTIVITY:</u>   Make a list of other places where noise pollution could be a problem.

Section 2 — Improving the Environment

Litter in Schools

People throw away lots of rubbish every day.
If we didn't do anything about it, there would be a big mess...

1 Finish the words to show some types of litter that get thrown away at school.

Fizzy drinks c....n   Newsp....p....r   Cr........p packet

Apple c....r....   Potato p........lings

2 The school wants some of the litter to be re-used. This is called recycling. Draw a circle round the correct words to show what can be done.

a) Glass bottles can be taken to a **BOTTLE BANK / RIVER**.

b) Newspapers and waste paper can be **COLLECTED AND RECYCLED / THROWN OUT OF THE WINDOW**.

c) Potato peelings can be put on **SANDWICHES / THE COMPOST HEAP**.

d) Cans can be **SAVED AND RECYCLED / DROPPED WHEN NO ONE IS LOOKING**.

3 Draw lines to match up the beginnings of the sentences with their correct endings. The sentences are about why recycling rubbish is a good idea.

If we keep throwing litter away	it pollutes the air with smoke.
Old papers and cardboard	can be melted and made into new ones.
Glass jars and bottles	we'll run out of space to put it.
If we burn rubbish	can be re-made into things like kitchen rolls.

Saving rubbish and recycling it is important. It helps to keep our environment clean.

Section 2 — Improving the Environment

Litter in Schools

Litter can be a big problem in schools because of all the people who go there every day.

1 Fill in the missing words in these sentences about litter. The words you need are on the litter bin.

When people throw litter on the floor, it looks ....

The proper place to put litter is in the ....

These help to keep the school .... and ....

litter bins
clean
tidy
messy

2 The children want to investigate the litter in their school. Tick 3 good questions for them to ask:

Hey! I'm the headmaster.

a) How many bins are there in the playground? ☐
b) How many bins are painted blue? ☐
c) Does every classroom have a bin? ☐
d) Who empties them? ☐

3 The children found a lot of litter in the bins, and on the playground surface. Circle the right words to finish off their writing.

There are **TOO MANY / NOT ENOUGH** bins.

The school needs **MORE / FEWER** bins in the playground.

Paper rubbish and old cans could be put in big plastic boxes for **MY DINNER / RECYCLING**.

ACTIVITY:
If we re-use rubbish instead of throwing it away, we can help keep the environment clean. Make a list of things that can be saved and recycled.

Section 2 — Improving the Environment

Improving the School Environment

Jim and Imran want to find out about the untidy patch of garden at school.
They think it could be made into a much nicer place.

1 The boys started with 3 questions, but the words got mixed up.
Write out their questions properly by putting the words in the right order.

a) the What garden does like? look

What ....

b) tell can we How nobody looks that it? after

How ....

c) we How make can garden the better? look

How ....

2 The sentences below describe what the boys decided to do.
Match the beginnings of the sentences with the correct endings.

Draw and label a picture	to show the muddy, trampled areas.
Take photos of the weeds	with rubber gloves on.
Collect all the rubbish	using a pencil and drawing book.
Draw a map	using a camera.
Describe how the garden looks	by writing using the computer.

(Draw and label a picture — using a pencil and drawing book.)

3 The picture below shows the litter Jim and Imran collected from the garden.
Write the words in this table to show the types of litter in order.

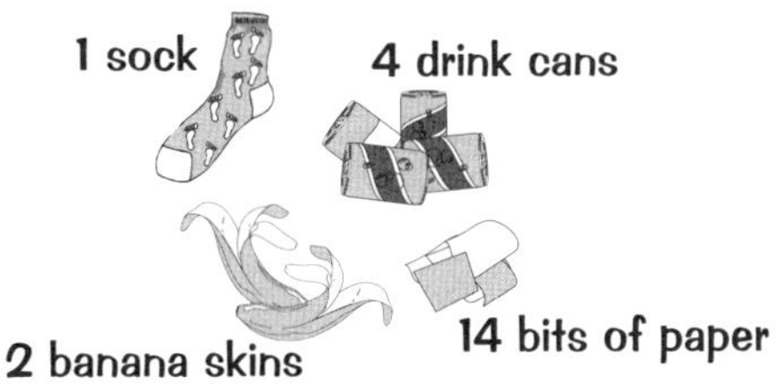

1 sock   4 drink cans

2 banana skins   14 bits of paper

14	
4	
2	
1	

There are lots of ways you can record how an area looks — like photos, maps, drawings...

Section 2 — Improving the Environment

Improving the School Environment

4 Jim and Imran asked their friends for ideas to improve the garden. Circle the right words in each of their ideas.

Pick up all the **LORRIES / LITTER**.

Use a **SPOON / SPADE** to dig the soil properly.

Plant trees and **FLOWERS / FISHFINGERS**.

Put a bench and a rubbish **BED / BIN** in the garden.

5 The sentences below are about the new and improved garden. Write YES if the sentence is right and NO if it's wrong.

The flowers make the garden smell horrible. ....

The garden looks more beautiful now. ....

The garden is well looked after, so there is more litter. ....

Birds and insects will visit the trees and flowers in the garden. ....

6 Put the words below into the table. Would they make a place look pretty or ugly?

OLD BOTTLES
FLOWERS   DIRT
CRISP PACKETS
TREES
DUCKS
POND

PRETTY	UGLY

DISCUSSION: Think about your local park. Does it have lots of litter? Does it have plants and trees? Does it need improving? If so, what would improve it?

Section 2 — Improving the Environment

Section 3 — Village Settlers

Early Settlers

Some of our towns and cities have been around for a very long time.
They all started much smaller than they are today, with just a few people living there.

1 Circle four items below that you think people would look for when starting a settlement hundreds of years ago.

- Water supplies
- Electricity
- Safety
- Chinese takeaway
- Flat land for crops
- Building materials
- Supermarkets

'Settling' just means 'setting up somewhere to live'.

2 Connect each feature to the reason why it was a good place to settle there.

Feature	Reason it was a good place to settle
Crossroad	Homes were safe and would not be destroyed.
Near a river	Middle meeting place for people.
Near a narrow part of a river	There was water nearby for cooking, drinking etc.
No chance of flooding	People from four different places could meet.
Between two large cities	People could get things across the river.

3 Use the descriptions below to help you put the right endings on the place names.

- **—ing** just means a settlement of people. E.g. Ketter**ing**
- **—ton** means the place of a house or farm. E.g. Bridling**ton**
- **—ham** means a small village. E.g. Grant**ham**

NOTTING............ (used to be a small village)
SOUTHAMP............ (used to be just a house or farm)
BIRMING............ (used to be a small village)
READ............ (the ending means 'a settlement')

ACTIVITY: Can you think of other place names that end in 'ing', 'ton' and 'ham'? Try to think of 5 places for each.

Evidence of Early Settlements

When you look at a map you can find out information about an area by looking at the place names.

1 Look at the map below and read the different place names.
Tick the word endings that can be found in place names on the map.

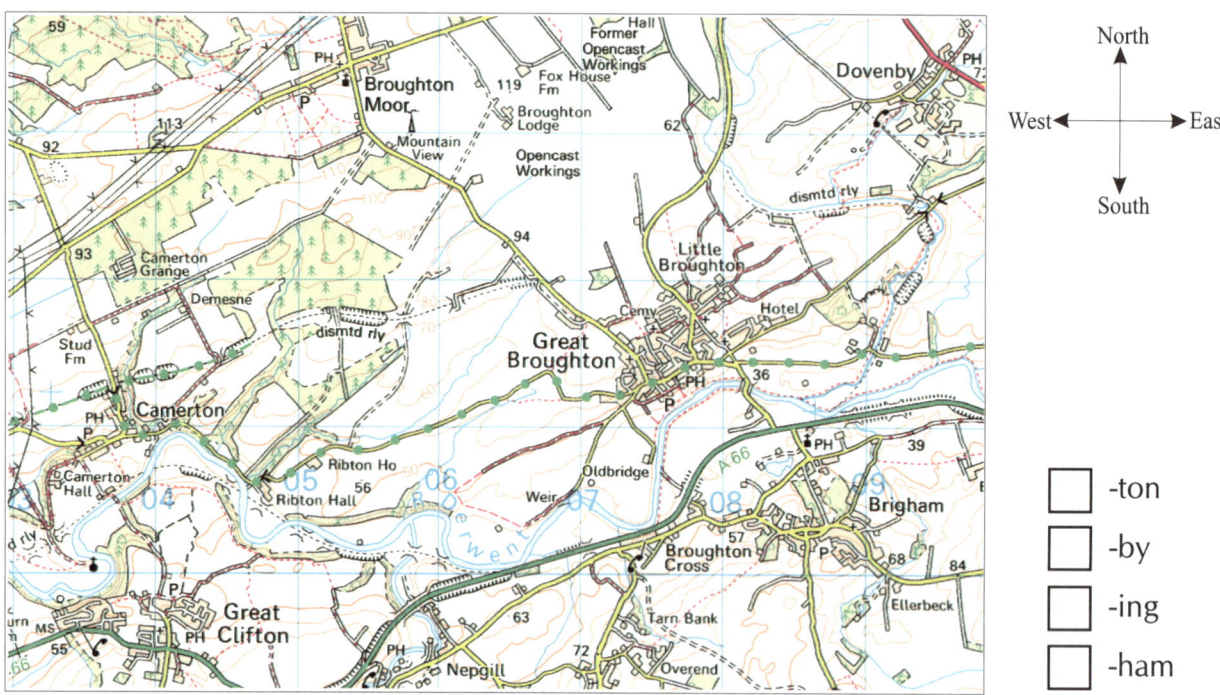

☐ -ton

☐ -by

☐ -ing

☐ -ham

2 The map shows an important feature which flows from east to west. It would have encouraged people to have settled there hundreds of years ago. Circle the feature below that is being described.

Runway for planes   River Derwent   The A66 road   River Nile

3 Tick the four reasons why people first settled in the places on the map.

☐ a) Great Clifton has a river crossing to get to the other side.

☐ b) Great Broughton has a river nearby for transport.

☐ c) Broughton Moor is at a crossroad.

☐ d) Dovenby is away from the river to protect from flooding.

☐ e) Camerton has a public telephone.

ACTIVITY: Think of some big towns or cities. Can you think of reasons why they were built in the places where they are? Use a map to help you.

Section 3 — Village Settlers

Villages Today

Little pictures (symbols) are used on maps to show what features a place has. All maps should have a key which tells you what each symbol means.

1 For each village below, tick the boxes under the features that are found there. Use the key and the map on the last page to help you.

Key

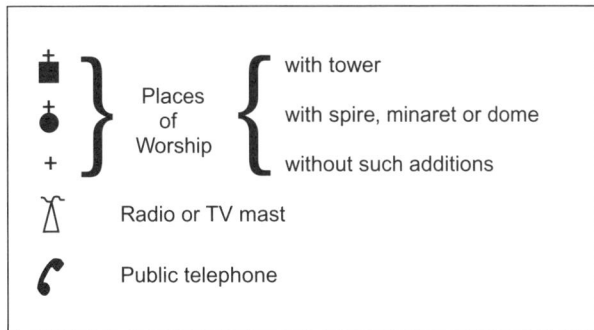

Features \ Villages	Public telephone	Church with tower	Church without spire or tower	Radio or TV mast
Broughton Cross				
Dovenby				
Broughton Moor				
Brigham				

2 The signpost below has had its symbols broken off. Draw lines to connect the places to their symbols.

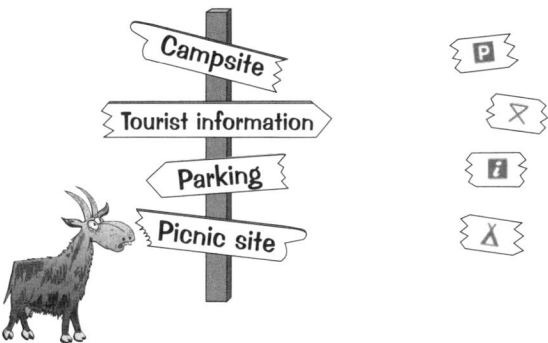

Maps use symbols to show what's there — use the key to find out what symbols mean.

Section 3 — Village Settlers

Finding Places and Getting There

It's important that we can find places on maps and work out how to get to places.
To find a place on a map we use numbers called <u>grid references</u>.

1 Use the map and key to work out the grid reference for each place below.

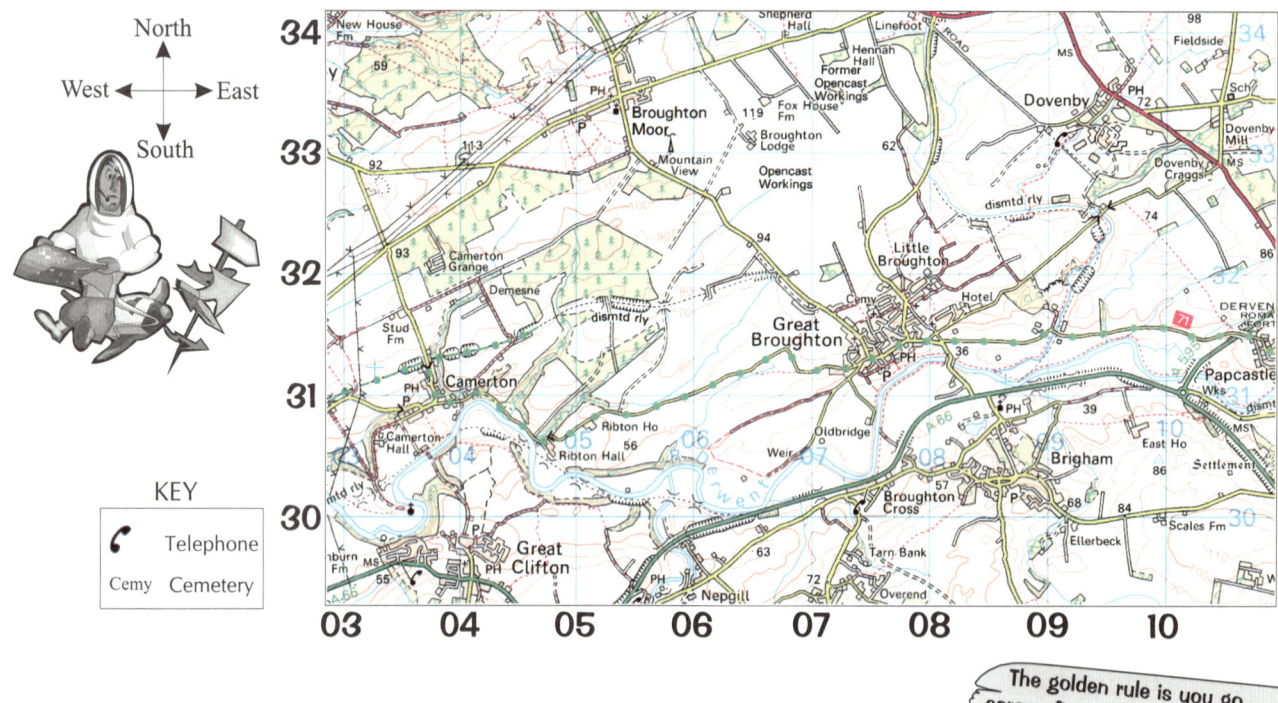

Cemetery   0731
Oldbridge   ....
Hotel   ....
Telephone in Dovenby ....
Camerton Hall   ....

Here's how to do it —
★ Find the cemetery on the map.
★ Then go along the bottom until you get to the line just before the cemetery — line 07.
★ Then go up the left-hand side until you get to the line just before the cemetery — 31.
★ Put 07 and 31 together to make the grid reference 0731.

The golden rule is you go across first and then up — just like you have to walk along the hall before you can go up the stairs.

2 Complete the directions from Great Clifton to Broughton Moor, choosing words from the box to fill in the gaps.

Take the A66 (the .... road) east towards Brigham.
Turn .... at Brigham towards Great Broughton.
Travel through Great Broughton.
Go past the .... and you will soon arrive at Broughton Moor.

| Opencast Workings |
| left |
| right   green |

ACTIVITY: Look at a map of your area. Find the grid references of your house, the pub nearest your house, your school and your local park.

Section 3 — Village Settlers

How Villages Develop

Settlements build up over time — they start simple and become more complicated as time goes on.

1 On this page, you are going to design your own village and show its development. Draw your village on the sketch below by following the instructions underneath.

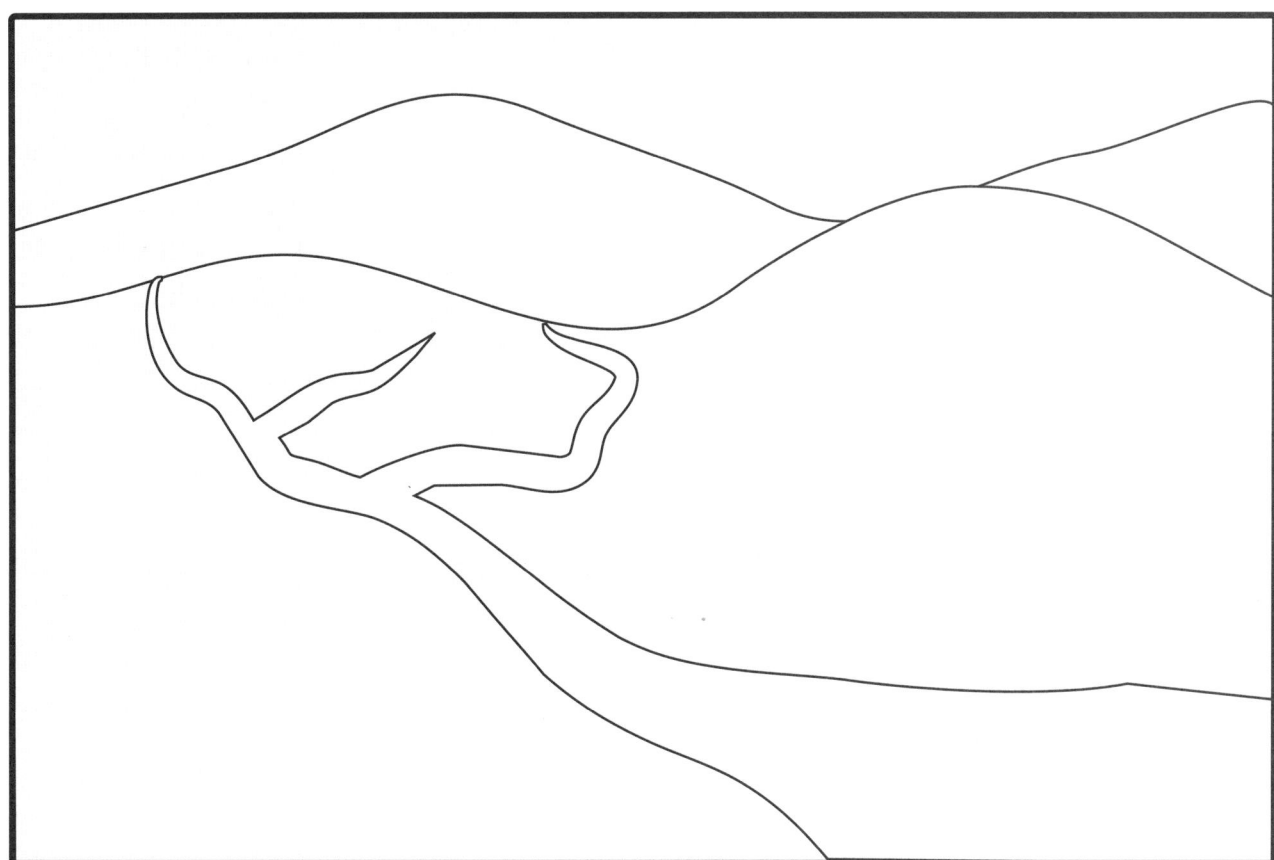

There are three stages to your village's development.
You need to draw each stage in order — and remember to use colour.
Make sure you don't make it too complicated.

 The settlement is built:

Add a few houses next to the river, then colour the river blue and the high ground green.

 The settlement grows into a village:

Add a few more houses, a simple road and bridge, and a church.

 The settlement grows bigger and has more services:

Add more houses, different roads, a pub and a post office.

It's not easy planning a settlement, so remember to keep it as simple as possible.

Section 4 — A Village in Kenya

Where is Kenya?

There are lots of countries in the world. You can find out where they are by looking at a world map.

1 Find Kenya on the world map and cross out the wrong words in the sentences.

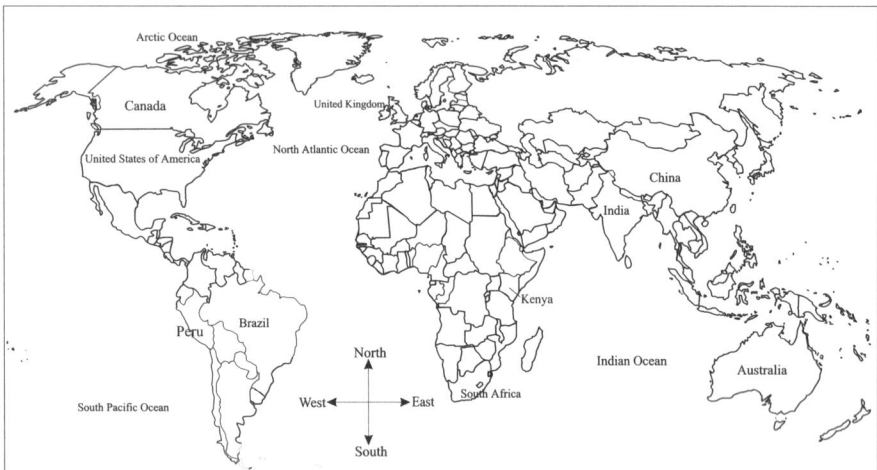

a) A country to the north of Kenya is **THE UK / BRAZIL**.

b) A country to the east of Kenya is **PERU / INDIA**.

c) Far away to the west of Kenya is **SOUTH AMERICA / AUSTRALIA**.

2 Put a tick in the box next to the CORRECT sentence.

☐ a) Australia is in the country of Kenya.
☐ b) Kenya is in the continent of Africa.

3 Are the sentences below about Kenya true?

Write **YES** if they are true and **NO** if they are not true.

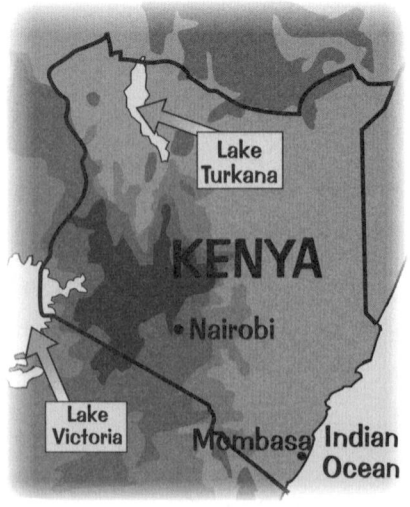

a) There are lakes in Kenya. ....
b) Kenya has a coastline. ....
c) Kenya has a big city called London. ....
d) Nairobi is a city in Kenya. ....
e) Mombasa is a city on the coast of Kenya. ....

ACTIVITY: Look at a world map. Find the name of a country beginning with the same letter as your name. Where in the world is that country?

Getting to Kenya

You can use maps to work out how to get to places.

1 Use words from the cloud to complete the pilot's description of flying to Kenya.

Words: Africa, France, airport, Mediterranean, Nairobi

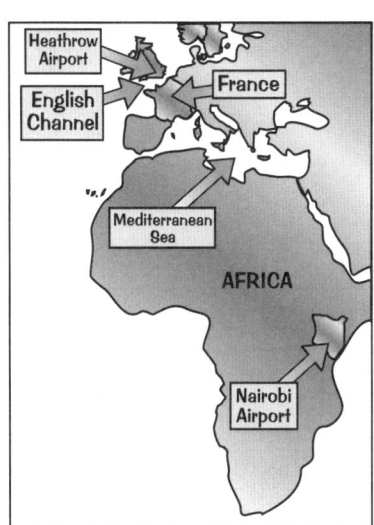

First I leave London's Heathrow ....
I cross the English Channel, and soon I am flying over
.... Then I cross the ....
Sea, and will soon fly over the continent of
.... Finally I land in Kenya's capital city,
....

2 Show the pilot's route to Kenya by following the instructions below.

Use the map in Q1 to help you.

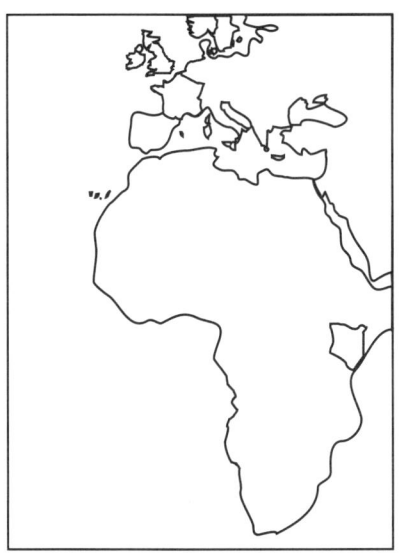

a) Colour the UK and Kenya in red, and label them.
b) Draw a small black dot in the UK to mark London, and label it.
c) Draw a small black dot in Kenya to mark Nairobi, and label it.
d) Draw a line with a ruler, joining up London and Nairobi, to show the pilot's route.

3 How far is it from the UK to Kenya? Draw a circle around the best answer.

just down the road   15 miles   150 miles   thousands of miles

Getting to Kenya by plane takes hours and hours — you couldn't walk there...

Section 4 — A Village in Kenya

A Kenyan Village

The photos show you a part of Kenya. You can see a village (1), and the landscape around it (2).

(1)  (2)

1 Look at photo (1). Draw circles round the correct words below.

a) The houses are **IN GROUPS / VERY FAR APART WITH BIG GARDENS**.
b) The roofs are **FLAT / ROUNDED AND MADE OF STRAW**.
c) The villagers are busy **PLAYING MARBLES / DRYING THEIR HARVEST IN THE SUN**.

2 Look at photo (2). Tick the three sentences that best describe the landscape.

☐ The sea can be seen.   ☐ There are only a few trees and plants.
☐ The soil looks bare and dry.   ☐ There are mountains with snow on them.
☐ It looks hot and sunny.   ☐ The area is covered in lush rainforest.

3 Which things in the picture below are natural and which are to do with people?

Human Features
(to do with people)

1. Mud wall
2. ....
3. ....

Physical Features
(natural)

1. ....
2. ....
3. ....

ACTIVITY: Draw a simple picture of your house and your street. Colour all the human features in red and the physical features in green. Which are there more of?

Section 4 — A Village in Kenya

Kenyan Homes and Schools

Kenyan and UK homes and schools are very different — but there are some similarities...

1 Look at the photos of Kenyan and UK houses. Are the sentences below true?

KENYA

UK

Write **YES** if they are true and **NO** if they are not true.

a) In both countries, houses are near to each other. ....
b) In both countries, the houses are tall with lots of windows. ....
c) In both countries, the homes have mud walls. ....

2 How are Kenyan and UK homes different?

Use the photos in Q1 to help you fill in the missing letters.

	Kenyan home	**UK home**
Windows	none or few windows	windows made of g................ss
Cooking	people cook o........ts..........e	people cook inside
Ground	made of e................th	pavements and roads

3 Look at the pictures of schools in Kenya and the UK. Circle the correct words in the sentences below.

KENYA

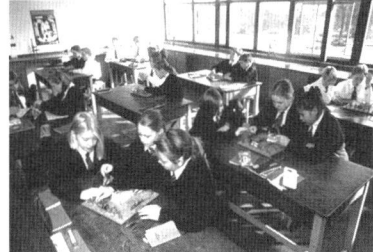
UK

In Kenya, pupils wear their own clothes for school, but in the UK pupils often wear **UNIFORMS / SPACESUITS**. In Kenya, the school can only afford a **COMPUTER / BLACKBOARD**, but in the UK children can work with expensive equipment.

Kenya is a very poor country, so its buildings and schools are much simpler than ours.

Section 4 — A Village in Kenya

Types of Work in the Village

The types of work that people do to earn money are called their 'economic activities'. The photos on this page show people working in the Kenyan village.

1 Tick the box next to the things that you can see in the photographs below.

- [ ] factory
- [ ] dust
- [ ] field of crops
- [ ] bare soil
- [ ] grazing land
- [ ] railway station

2 Draw lines to match up the beginnings of these sentences about the villagers' economic activities with their correct endings.

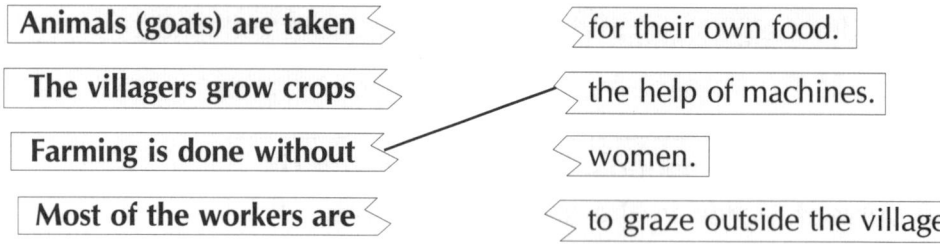

Animals (goats) are taken	for their own food.
The villagers grow crops	the help of machines.
Farming is done without	women.
Most of the workers are	to graze outside the village.

3 Circle the correct words in the sentences below.

a) Farmers in **KENYA AND THE UK / KENYA ONLY** grow crops and keep animals.

b) A lot of work done in Kenya is **GROWING CROPS AND KEEPING ANIMALS / MAKING THINGS IN FACTORIES**.

c) In the UK, most people work **INDOORS / OUTSIDE** (e.g. factory and office workers, doctors). In Kenya, most people work **OUTSIDE / UNDERWATER**.

ACTIVITY: Make a list of as many economic activities as you can that we have in the UK.

Selling and Trading in Kenya

People buy and sell things in markets and shops. This is called trading. The photos below show markets in Kenya and the UK.

1 Look at the photos below. Complete the sentences below by drawing circles around the correct words.

Markets in Kenya and the UK have many similarities. In both Kenya and the UK:

a) The market stalls are **OUTSIDE / INDOORS**.
b) People can buy **A TV / THINGS PRODUCED BY FARMERS**.
c) People need **MONEY / CRISPS** to buy the goods.

2 The following passage is about the differences between Kenyan and UK markets. Fill in the gaps using the words below.

In Kenya, people sell their own spare ....,
but in the UK shops buy their goods from other places.
In Kenya, the market is the main place to buy food, but in the UK most people go to a ....
In Kenya, the market is in an open space without buildings, but in the UK it is in the .... with the shops.

3 Draw lines to match up the 2 halves of these sentences about markets and shops.

Unlike shops, market stalls	like washing machines.
Some shops sell big expensive things	are not there all the time.
In a Kenyan market, people mainly sell	spare crops that they've grown themselves.

In Kenya, most people go to markets to buy and sell things, rather than to shops...

Section 4 — A Village in Kenya

Selling and Trading in Kenya

In Kenya, people have to travel to the markets from where they live.

1 Unscramble these words that describe how people in Kenya get to market.

People don't go by **LDSEEG**. ....SLEDGE..........

Most people **LAWK**. ....

Some people might have a **TRAC**, or a **KIBE**. ....

A few people may travel by **RAC**. ....

2 Match up the 2 halves of these descriptions of where people in a Kenyan village go to shop:

People often walk to a market — to a town to buy clothes.

People sometimes go by bus — like Nairobi.

People hardly ever shop in far-away cities — which is not far away.

3 Look at the food for sale in the photo below. Circle the two foods that Kenyans eat a lot of.

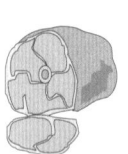 HAM

 SAUSAGES

 CHEESEBURGERS

 SANDWICHES

 VEGETABLES

 FRUIT

ACTIVITY: Make a list of all the things you need to buy in order to live. Then make a list of all the things you would buy if you had enough money.

Section 4 — A Village in Kenya

Section 5 — What's in the News?

International News

The word 'news' comes from 'new stories'. International news is news that's from all over the world.

1 Headlines tell us what news stories are about. Draw lines to match up each headline to its story.

HEADLINES

Police chase armed robbers

Worst bush fires for 10 years

Fears about the French countryside

Help offered to African country

NEWS STORIES

Thousands of new houses are to be built in the French countryside.

The American president promised money for schools in Kenya.

Expensive jewellery was stolen from a museum.

Flames and smoke can be seen over parts of Australia.

2 Unscramble the messed-up words to find the names of 3 countries from the news stories in Q1.

YENKA ....
RECNAF ....
RATIASULA ....

3 Headlines in newspapers have to be short and snappy. Read the stories below and write a headline for each of them.

Headline

....

....

Hundreds of workers today were trying to stop oil polluting the beaches of Spain, following yesterday's accident. Two oil tanker ships collided, spilling oil into the sea...

....

Local people, who are poor farmers and fishermen, may lose their land and homes on a tiny island in the Caribbean. The area is to become a holiday resort, with expensive hotels and swimming pools.

ACTIVITY: Make a list of all the things that you find in newspapers, apart from news.

International News

When a country is hit by disaster, it becomes a news story, both at home and abroad.

1 Use the words in the cloud to complete the news reports below.

a) Months of no rain in parts of Ethiopia have caused .... and starvation.

b) In northern India, hundreds of people are dead after buildings collapsed in an ....

c) Hundreds of square miles are underwater following the .... in Bangladesh.

d) Today smoke, ash and lava were pouring out of Mount Etna, a .... in Sicily.

floods, volcano, earthquake, drought

2 Write a newspaper report, with a headline, about the flooding you can see in the photos below.

....
....
....
....
....
....
....

Hints: The floods happened in Colorado, America after weeks of heavy rain. What has happened to the ground, houses, trees and cars? What will the people be doing? What will it be like to try and rescue people and animals?

DISCUSSION: Can you think of any natural disasters that have happened recently?

Section 5 — What's in the News?

Local News

Local papers, local radio stations, TV and local websites — all tell you the latest news for your area.

1 Read this article from a local paper, and then answer the questions.

> The go-ahead has been given to build the new bypass around the village of Snoringham. This new road will take a lot of the traffic around, instead of through, the village, and many local people are pleased about it. But, some people from this area think the bypass is a bad idea.

a) Make up a headline for the story.
   (Remember, it should be short and snappy.)

   ....
   ....
   ....

b) What is a bypass?

   ....
   ....

c) Is everyone pleased about the bypass?

   ....

2 Below are 3 people's opinions (what they thought) about the bypass. Write in the spaces who you think said what, choosing from:

PC Stoppit the policeman   **Mr Hay** the farmer   **Mr Twigg** the wildlife expert

a) "I will lose some of my best fields."   ....

b) "The village streets will be much safer."   ....

c) "Trees, wild plants and animals will disappear."   ....

3 People might have different opinions about the bypass.
Circle the correct words below to complete these statements.

I think the bypass is a good idea. The village streets will be a lot **NOISIER / QUIETER** and there will be **FEWER / MORE** accidents.

I think the bypass is a bad idea. The environment will be **IMPROVED / DAMAGED** and the air will be **POLLUTED / CLEANER**.

News stories give people information and make them think and form opinions.

Section 5 — What's in the News?

Weather News

Weather maps and forecasts tell us the latest news about the weather.
At any time, in the UK or across the world, the weather is different in different places.

1) Circle the correct words in these messages from travellers:

a) "For my holidays this year I spent a week in the **SUN / SNOW** in Spain, then a week skiing in the snow in **SWEDEN / PORTUGAL**."

b) "It was sunny as I left my car, but when I reached the top of the mountains there was **SNOW / COTTON WOOL** on top."

c) "It's raining heavily by the **SEA / SUN** in western Scotland, but Jim says it's dry in London."

2) Symbols (simple pictures) are used on weather maps. In the boxes below, draw a symbol that you think shows:

sunny weather	cloudy weather	rain

3) Write 'CLIMATE' or 'WEATHER' against each of these descriptions:

CLIMATE = how warm / wet / windy etc. a place usually is every year.
WEATHER = the day-to-day changes.

a) In Kenya, half the year is always dry, and the other half is rainy. ....
b) Winters in northern Canada are colder than winters in the UK. ....
c) After rain tonight, tomorrow will be drier and sunnier. ....
d) It snowed last week, but the sun has melted it all away now. ....

We can find out about the weather beFORE it happens, from the FOREcast.

Section 5 — What's in the News?

31

Weather and Travel News

Television and radio tell us the news about the weather and driving conditions during the day.

1 Match up the beginnings and endings of these sentences about TV weather forecasts.

We are shown a map — to tell us about temperatures, rain and wind.
We are shown symbols and numbers — of unusual weather, e.g. snow or floods.
We are sometimes shown videos — to show us <u>where</u> the presenter is talking about.

2 Circle the correct words in these sentences about TV weather forecasts.

Viewers can look at coloured maps of the UK, with **COLD / WARM** areas coloured blue or green, and **COLD / WARM** areas coloured red or yellow.

Arrows are drawn on maps to show us which way the wind is blowing.
The bigger the arrows, the **WETTER / STRONGER** the wind is.

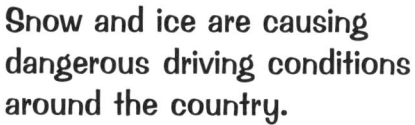
...raining cats and dogs over areas of southern England...

3 Radio reports help travellers to know where it is safe to go. What should drivers do when they hear this radio report?

Snow and ice are causing dangerous driving conditions around the country.

Tick the boxes to show the best answers

☐ Stop and cry
☐ Speed up and drive dangerously
☐ Slow down and drive very carefully
☐ Avoid making unnecessary journeys
☐ Eat a banana

<u>DISCUSSION:</u>   Some people need to know what the weather will be like more than others. Which people might have jobs that are affected by the weather?

Section 5 — What's in the News?

Section 6 — Connecting to the World

Sending Faxes

A fax is a copy of something that's sent through the phone lines. You send it from your fax machine to someone else's by dialling their 'fax number'. The copy is printed out by their machine.

1 The children at the village school on the map want to deliver party invitations to children at other schools.

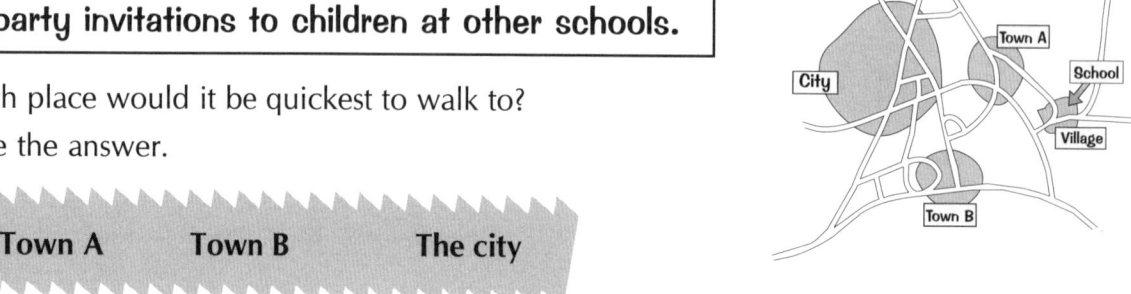

a) Which place would it be quickest to walk to? Circle the answer.

    Town A   Town B   The city

b) Write these ways of sending the invitations in order of speed.

    By post   **Take a note to each school by car**   **Send each school a fax**

Fastest ➡ 1. ....

2. ....

Slowest ➡ 3. ....

2 This table shows how many faxes were sent to the village school in one week.

Faxes to the School

	from Town A	from Town B	from City
from other schools	10	12	24
from bookshops	6		12
from other businesses		5	6
TOTAL	20	24	

a) Fill in the missing numbers in the table.

b) Tick the other businesses that would probably fax the school.

☐ Paper suppliers   ☐ Car factory
☐ Pub   ☐ Food suppliers

Schools, shops and other businesses can send information very quickly by fax.

Sending E-mails

E-mails are messages that are typed and sent using a computer.
To write to someone, you need to know their e-mail address.

1 Here are some good and bad things about e-mail. Shade in the GOOD things.

- An e-mail can be sent very quickly.
- E-mails travel very quickly to far-away places.
- You can't e-mail someone who hasn't got a computer.
- E-mails don't need stamps.
- E-mails don't have to be posted, sorted and sent by train, boat or plane.
- E-mails aren't untidy like some people's handwriting.
- E-mails can't be sent in a power cut.
- Parcels can't be sent by e-mail.

2 Draw lines to match up each type of message to a good way of sending it.

Write to a friend in hospital — Card

Wish your uncle 'happy birthday' for next week — E-mail

Tell someone what time you will meet them tomorrow — Letter

3 You are writing an e-mail about your local area.
Circle the correct words in the sentences about attachments.

Attachments are extra pages that are sent out with e-mails.

a) You could attach a **MAP / MENU** to show where the school is in the village.

b) You could attach a **PHOTO / BOOK** to show what the shops look like.

c) You could attach a **BAR GRAPH / FROG** to show how many different types of houses there are.

E-mails are quick to send and the computer can even check the spelling...

Section 6 — Connecting to the World

Making a Journey

Many people from the UK now travel to places all over the world for holidays.

1 Write the letters on the map to show where each holiday is in the world.

- **A.** A wildlife safari holiday in Kenya.
- **B.** A seaside holiday in Spain.
- **C.** A trip to EuroDisney in France.

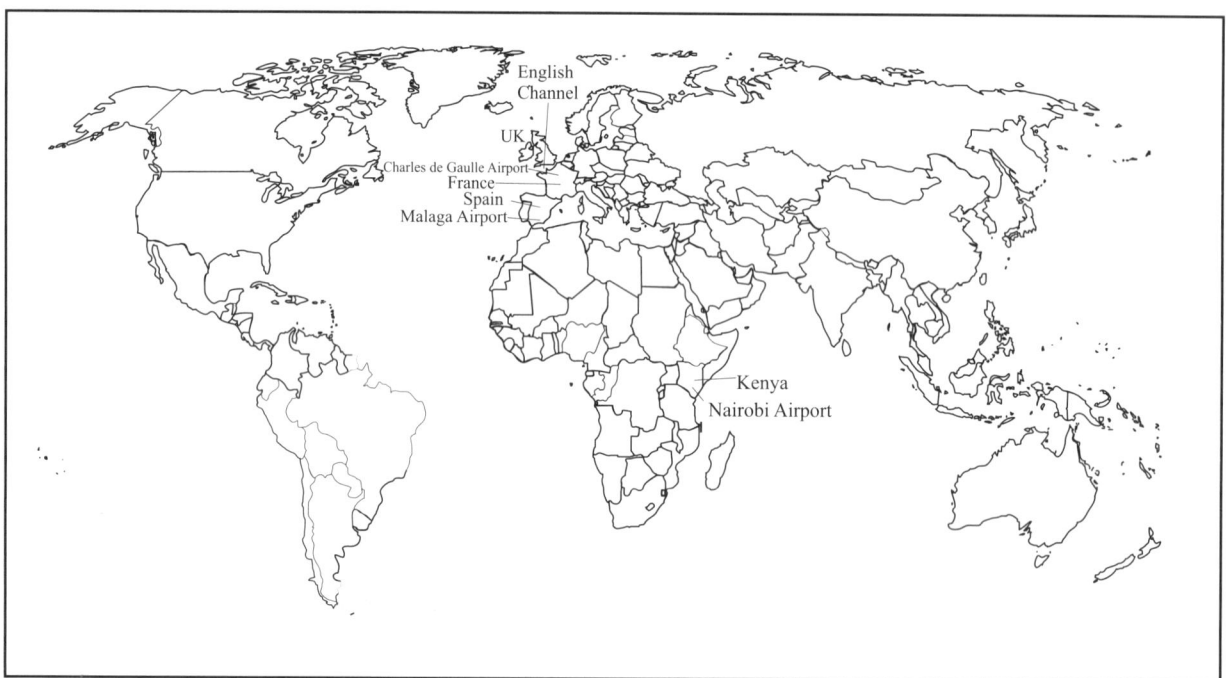

2 Which airport would you land at if you went to the countries below?

Use the map to help you.

The airport is
....

The airport is
....

The airport is
....

3 Sam flew from the UK to Spain. Complete his postcard using the words below.

Dear Mum,
We flew .... over the .... Channel.
Then we flew over ....
At last we landed in Spain at .... airport.

Malaga   France   south   English

A world map or a globe shows where you live in the world and where other countries are...

Section 6 — Connecting to the World

Making a Journey

Computers can help us find out facts about other places, and ways of getting to them.
Raj wants help in planning a holiday to Australia.

1 How can Raj find out about how to get to Sydney? Circle the correct answers.

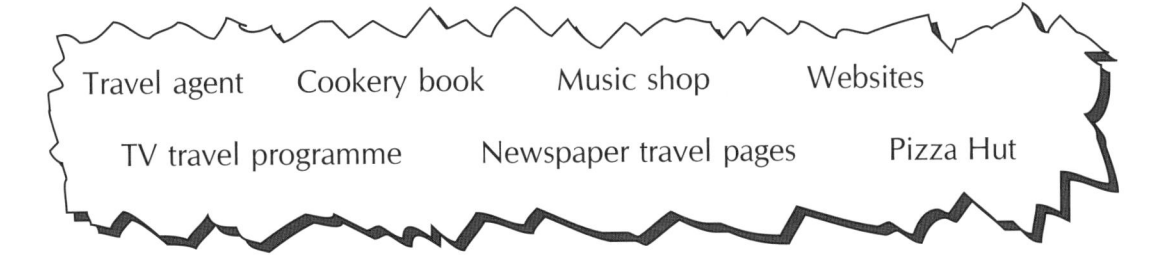

Travel agent   Cookery book   Music shop   Websites

TV travel programme   Newspaper travel pages   Pizza Hut

2 Raj wants to plan his ITINERARY (his route and how long it will take). Tick the three useful questions for him to ask a travel agent.

- [ ] Which airports in the UK have flights to Australia?
- [ ] Do people in Sydney like chips?
- [ ] How many hours will the journey take?
- [ ] Which places do we call at during the journey?

3 Draw a line on the map to show Raj's flight from the UK to Sydney. He goes from LONDON to DUBAI, then to SINGAPORE, then to SYDNEY.

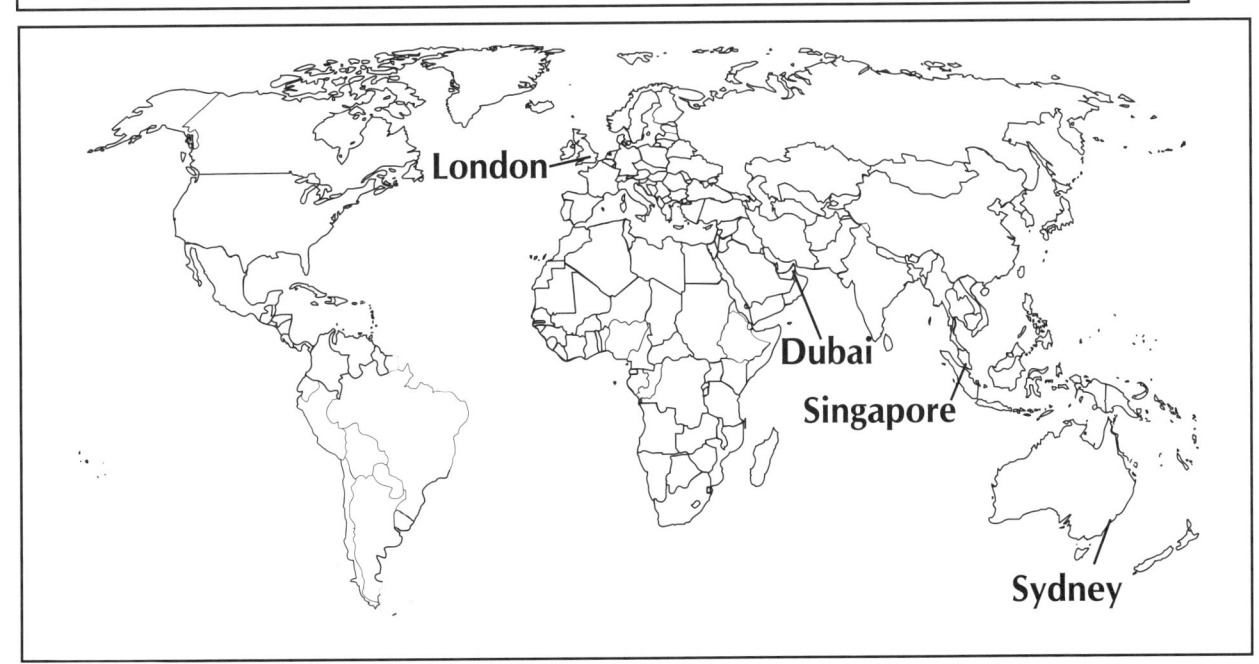

London — Dubai — Singapore — Sydney

ACTIVITY: Find Paris on a map. Plan a way of getting from your house to a hotel in Paris using as many different types of transport as you can think of.
(e.g. you could walk to the bus stop, then get a bus to town, then...)

Section 6 — Connecting to the World

Different Activities

Activities are things that people do. There are lots of different activities — like doing sums, playing with toys, swimming...

1 Here are the activities that Sally did yesterday. Circle the answers to the questions.

9 am - 12	morning school
12 - 1 pm	lunch and play
1 - 3 pm	afternoon school
4 - 5 pm	teatime and TV
6 - 7 pm	swimming
7 - 8 pm	homework
8 pm	reading then sleeping

a) How long was morning school?
   3 hours / one hour

b) How long was afternoon school?
   one hour / 2 hours

c) How long did Sally do homework for?
   3 hours / one hour

2 Draw lines to match these words to their meanings.

Word	Meaning
WORK	Doing something for fun in your spare time.
LEISURE TIME	Doing jobs or being at school.
RECREATION	Free time, when you can do whatever you want.

3 Put these activities under the correct headings.

watching TV   riding a bike   doing sums
playing football   homework   history lesson

Work	Leisure
....	....
....	....
....	....

ACTIVITY:
1. Write a list of all the activities you did yesterday.
2. Now decide which of them were work and which were leisure.

Making a Questionnaire

Chetan decided to find out about the activities the children in his class do.
He made a list of questions to ask — this is called a questionnaire.

1 Unscramble the words to find out what Chetan needed to think about first.

a) do | What | I | find | want | to | out?

What ....?

b) shall | ask? | I | Who

Who ....?

c) ask? | I | people | How | many | shall

How ....?

2 How many children should Chetan ask? Circle the 2 best answers.

- 1 boy and 1 girl
- all the children in his class
- all the children in the world
- his dog
- the 5 children on his table

3 Match up the questions with their answers.

Did you play football on Monday? — In the park.

How long did you play for? — Yes.

Where did you play football? — One hour.

ACTIVITY:
1. Write down three questions you could ask to find out about the activities other children do.
2. Try them out on your friends.

Section 7 — How Do We Spend Our Time?

Where Do Activities Happen?

The table below shows what Chetan found out from the children on his table.

1 Use Chetan's table of results to answer the questions.

	Chetan	Gareth	Kate	Laura	Mark
Hours working at school	5	5	5	5	5
Hours watching TV	1	2	1	0.5	0.5
Hours playing football	0	1	0	0	1
Where I played football	-	RG	-	-	RG
Hours playing tennis	0	0	0	1	0
Where I played tennis	-	-	-	TC	-
Hours doing homework	1	0	1	1	1
Hours doing judo	1	1	0	0	0
Where I did judo	C	C	-	-	-
Hours on my bike	1	1	1	0	0
Where I rode my bike	P	P	P	-	-

KEY
RG   Recreation Ground
TC   Tennis Courts
C   College
P   Park

a) How many children watched TV? ....

b) Where did Gareth and Mark play football?
....

c) Who went to Judo?
....

d) Who didn't do any homework?
....

2 Draw symbols (little pictures) on the map to show where the children did these activities.

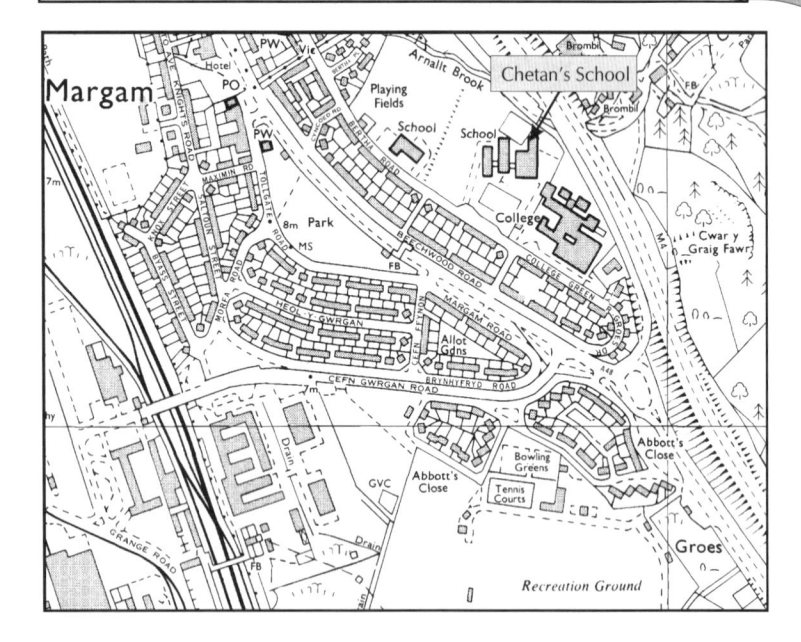

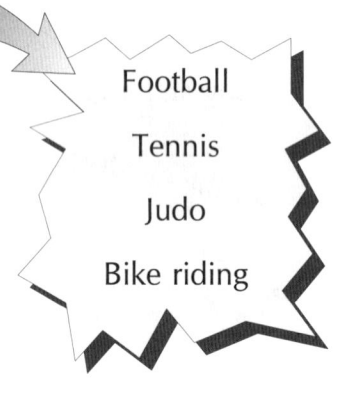

Football
Tennis
Judo
Bike riding

E.g. For football, you could draw a little football like this — ⚽

3 Put your symbols in the boxes to make a key for the map.

☐ Football   ☐ Judo   ☐ Tennis   ☐ Bike riding

Chetan's questionnaire helped him find out what people did and where they did it.

Section 7 — How Do We Spend Our Time?

What Activities Do We Do?

The results table can be used to work out more facts about what the children do.

	Chetan	Gareth	Kate	Laura	Mark
Hours working at school	5	5	5	5	5
Hours watching TV	1	2	1	0.5	0.5
Hours playing football	0	1	0	0	1
Where I played football	-	RG	-	-	RG
Hours playing tennis	0	0	0	1	0
Where I played tennis	-	-	-	TC	-
Hours doing homework	1	0	1	1	1
Hours doing judo	1	1	0	0	0
Where I did judo	C	C	-	-	-
Hours on my bike	1	1	1	0	0
Where I rode my bike	P	P	P	-	-

KEY
- RG   Recreation Ground
- TC   Tennis Courts
- C   College
- P   Park

1 Circle the answers to these questions.

a) Who spent 5 hours in total on work activities?   **GARETH / KATE**

b) How long did all the other children spend on work activities?   **5 HOURS / 6 HOURS**

2 Shade in the hobbies.

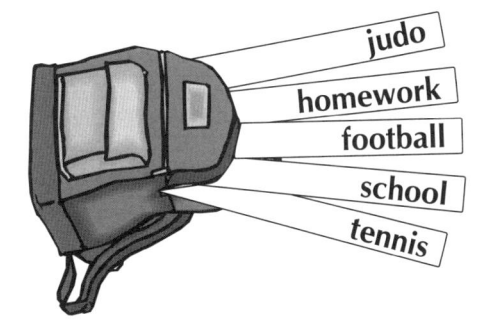

- judo
- homework
- football
- school
- tennis

3 All the children watched TV in their leisure time.
Follow these instructions to find the AVERAGE time spent watching TV.

a) Add up all the hours spent watching TV.   .... hours.

b) Divide this by the number of children (5) to get the average.   .... hour(s).

ACTIVITY:

1. Ask all the children in your class what their favourite activity is.
2. Count how many children like each activity.
3. Draw a bar chart showing the favourite activities — don't forget to label it.
4. Which activity do most children like best?

Section 7 — How Do We Spend Our Time?

Weather and Activities

The weather affects a lot of activities. A day at the beach is better when it's sunny, and driving to work can be scary when it's foggy.

1 Choose words from the cloud to complete these sentences.

a) The farmer was pleased it was .... so that he could harvest his crops.

b) James wanted .... weather so that he could fly a kite.

c) We were pleased that there was lots of .... for skiing.

d) I took an umbrella when I went for a walk, because of the ....

Cloud words: snow, windy, cats and dogs, rain, cloudy, dry

2 Match up the 2 halves of each sentence.

It rained all night	so they closed the airport because the pilots couldn't see.
It was very foggy	so the builders couldn't work on our roof.
It was very windy	so the football pitch was flooded.

3 Unscramble the muddled-up words to finish these sentences.

a) "When we got to the tennis match, it was cancelled because it was **GRINAIN**." ....

b) "Our picnic at the seaside was spoiled because there was a **LOCD DNIW**." ....

c) "We couldn't go out in our boat because it was **GOFGY**." ....

Ooops. Stepped in a poodle.

ACTIVITY:
Draw pictures of activities you like to do —
a) When it is raining.   b) When it is sunny and warm.   c) When it is snowy.

Section 7 — How Do We Spend Our Time?

The Answers

Section 1 — Investigating the Local Area

Page 1

Q1 UK should be coloured red:

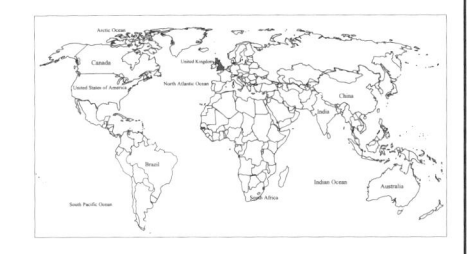

Q2 country; counties; south-east.
Q3 a) cross
   b) tick
   c) tick
   d) tick

Page 2

Q1 a) a pub
   b) a house
   c) a church
Q2 road, bridge.
Q3 In order, the missing words are: trees; green; river; hill.

Page 3

Q1 Red line should be drawn around the built-up area and around the pub; farmland should be coloured brown and woodland coloured green:

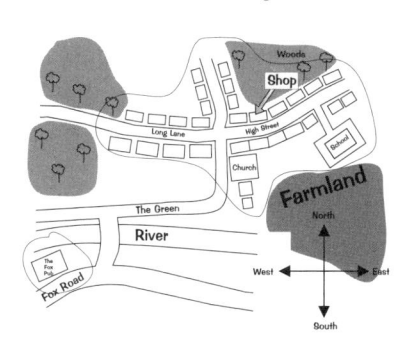

Q2 The pub — built as a place to stay....
   The houses — built close together around the church.......
   The church — in the centre of the village.
   The school — on the edge of the village....
   The shops — on the main street where lots of people go.
Q3 flood; attractive; soils.

Page 4

Q1 Houses should be coloured red; services (hairdresser, bank, PO, school, church) — yellow; shop — blue; woodland — green; farmland — brown; roads — black:

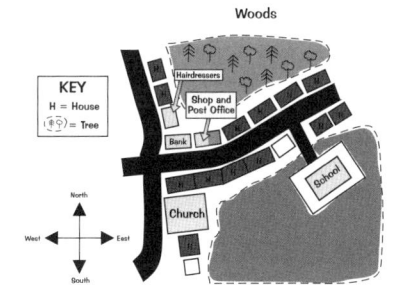

Q2 How many houses are there? 13
   How many services are there? 5 (hairdresser, bank, PO, church, school)
   How many shops are there? 1
Q3

Page 5

Q1 farmer; hairdresser; teacher; vicar.
Q2 a) to city C
   b) to town B
   c) to city C
   d) in town A.
Q3 a) to the village
   b) to the city
   c) to the village
   d) to the city
   e) to the town

Page 6

Q1 a), c) and d) should be copied out.
Q2 a) TARMAC
      GRASS
   b) QUIETER
   c) DIRTIER
   d) FEWER
Q3 In order, the missing words are: quiet; traffic; lorries; safer; dangerous; fresh; pollution.

Page 7

Q1 A — housing estate
   B — factory
   C — road
Q2 a) count
   b) picture
   c) photograph
   d) factory
Q3 pictures of a bird; rabbit; stream; flower

Page 8

Q1 In order, the missing words are: wood; houses; animals; narrow.
Q2 a) 50 YEARS AGO
   b) TODAY
   c) TODAY
   d) 50 YEARS AGO
   e) TODAY
Q3 more noise;
   fewer wild animals;
   more traffic;
   more pollution

The Answers

The Answers

Section 2 — Improving the Environment

Page 9

Q1 Playing football on the playing field — Trampled, muddy grass.
Parked cars waiting to collect children — Blocked roads and traffic jams.
Eating packed lunches and snacks — Litter on the ground.

Q2 a) WATER pollution
b) AIR pollution
c) AIR pollution
d) NOISE pollution

Q3 In order, the missing words are: buses; playtime; neighbours; drains; stream.

Page 10

Q1 1. singing
2. shouting
3. clinking knives and forks
4. talking
5. cars

Q2 1. Classroom — working
2. Dining Hall — eating
3. Library — quiet reading
4. Playground — playing

Q3 very noisy — playground
quite noisy — dining hall
quite quiet — classroom
very quiet — library

Page 11

Q1 Fizzy drinks can; Newspaper; Crisp packet; Apple core; Potato peelings.

Q2 a) bottle bank
b) collected and recycled
c) the compost heap
d) saved and recycled

Q3 If we keep throwing litter away — we'll run out of space to put it.
Old papers and cardboard — can be re-made into things like kitchen rolls.
Glass jars and bottles — can be melted and made into new ones.
If we burn rubbish — it pollutes the air with smoke.

Page 12

Q1 In order, the missing words are: messy; litter bins; clean/tidy; tidy/clean.

Q2 a), c) and d) should be ticked.

Q3 not enough; more; recycling.

Page 13

Q1 a) What does the garden look like?
b) How can we tell that nobody looks after it?
c) How can we make the garden look better?

Q2 Take photos of the weeds — using a camera.
Collect all the rubbish — with rubber gloves on.
Draw a map — to show the muddy, trampled areas.
Describe how the garden looks — by writing using the computer.

Q3 14 bits of paper
4 drink cans
2 banana skins
1 sock

Page 14

Q4 litter; spade; flowers; bin.
Q5 no, yes, no, yes.
Q6 PRETTY — flowers, trees, ducks, pond.
UGLY — old bottles, dirt, crisp packets.

Section 3 — Village Settlers

Page 15

Q1 water supplies; flat land for crops; building materials; safety

Q2 Near a river — There was water nearby for cooking, drinking etc.
Near a narrow part of a river — People could get things across the river.
No chance of flooding — Homes were safe and would not be destroyed.
Between two large cities — Middle meeting place for people.

Q3 Nottingham
Southampton
Birmingham
Reading

Page 16

Q1 -ton; -by; -ham
Q2 River Derwent.
Q3 a), b), c) and d) should be ticked.

Page 17

Q1 Broughton Cross — telephone;
Dovenby — telephone;
Broughton Moor — church with tower, church without spire or tower, radio or TV mast;
Brigham — church with tower, church without spire or tower.

Q2 P Parking
   ⚔ Picnic site
   i Tourist information
   ⋀ Campsite

Page 18

Q1 Oldbridge   0730
   Hotel   0831
   Telephone   0933
   Camerton Hall 0330

Q2 In order, the missing words are: green; left; Opencast Workings.

Page 19

Q1 Maps should show the development as suggested in a, b and c, as well as an appropriate key.
a) A few houses next to the river, with the river coloured blue and the high ground green.
b) A few more houses, a simple road and bridge, and a church.
c) More houses, different roads, a pub and a post office.

Section 4 — A Village in Kenya

Page 20

Q1 a) A country to the north of Kenya is the UK.
    b) A country to the east of Kenya is India.
    c) Far away to the west of Kenya is South America.
Q2 'Kenya is in the continent of Africa' should be ticked.
Q3 a) YES
    b) YES
    c) NO
    d) YES
    e) YES

Page 21

Q1 In order, the missing words are: airport; France; Mediterranean; Africa; Nairobi.
Q2 The UK and Kenya should be coloured red and labelled. London and Nairobi should be marked, labelled and joined together, as shown:

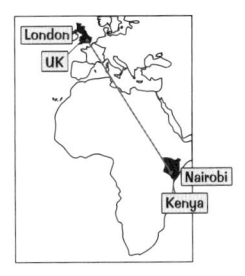

Q3 Thousands of miles.

Page 22

Q1 a) in groups
    b) rounded and made of straw
    c) drying their harvest in the sun
Q2 'There are only a few trees and plants.', 'The soil looks bare and dry.', and 'It looks hot and sunny.' should be ticked.
Q3 Human features — thatched roof; well.
    Physical features — bare earth; wild animal; tree.

Page 23

Q1 a) YES
    b) NO
    c) NO
Q2 Kenyan home — people cook outside; ground made of earth.
    UK home — windows made of glass.
Q3 uniforms; blackboard.

Page 24

Q1 'dust', 'grazing land', 'field of crops' and 'bare soil' should be ticked.
Q2 Animals (goats) are taken — to graze outside the village.
    The villagers grow crops — for their own food.
    Most of the workers are — women.
Q3 a) Kenya and the UK
    b) growing crops and keeping animals
    c) indoors; outside.

Page 25

Q1 a) outside
    b) things produced by farmers
    c) money
Q2 In order, the missing words are: crops; supermarket; town centre.
Q3 Unlike shops, market stalls — are not there all the time.
    Some shops sell big expensive things — like washing machines.
    In a Kenyan market, people mainly sell — spare crops that they've grown themselves.

Page 26

Q1 Most people WALK. Some people might have a CART, or a BIKE. A few people may travel by CAR.
Q2 People often walk to a market — which is not far away.
    People sometimes go by bus — to a town to buy clothes.
    People hardly ever shop in far-away cities — like Nairobi.
Q3 fruit; vegetables.

Section 5 — What's in the News?

Page 27

Q1 Police chase armed robbers — Expensive jewellery was stolen from a museum.
    Worst bush fires for 10 years — Flames and smoke can be seen over parts of Australia.
    Fears about the French countryside — Thousands of new houses are to be built in the French countryside.
    Help offered to African country — The American president promised money for schools in Kenya.
Q2 Kenya; France; Australia.
Q3 The headlines should be very short and should quickly sum up the news story.
    For example, 'Pollution Fears After Oil Tankers Collide'; 'Holiday Resort Threatens Land and Homes'.

Page 28

Q1 a) drought
    b) earthquake
    c) floods
    d) volcano
Q2 As an example, your report could sound like this:
    Headline — Flooding Destroys Homes In Colorado.
    Main report — Many square miles of Colorado are underwater today, in the area's worst floods for 30 years. Several weeks of heavy rain have caused rivers to overflow, so that homes, trees, fields and roads are underwater. People's carpets, furniture, gardens and cars are all damaged by the water. Most people have moved to drier areas, with things that they managed to save. Police and the Fire Service have used boats to rescue trapped people, pets and farm animals.
    Two elderly people were carried to safety last night by helicopter. The cost of this disaster will be millions of dollars.

The Answers

Page 29

Q1 a) Your headline could be like this — 'Bypass to go ahead'.
 b) A bypass is a road that goes around, not through the middle of, a place.
 c) No.
Q2 a) Mr Hay
 b) PC Stoppit
 c) Mr Twigg
Q3 In order, the correct words are: quieter; fewer; damaged; polluted.

Page 30

Q1 a) sun; Sweden
 b) snow
 c) sea
Q2 Symbols could be:
 a round sun for sunny weather;
 a fluffy cloud for cloudy weather;
 some raindrops for rain.
Q3 a) climate
 b) climate
 c) weather
 d) weather

Page 31

Q1 We are shown a map — to show us where the presenter is talking about.
 We are shown symbols and numbers — to tell us about temperatures, rain and wind.
 We are sometimes shown videos — of unusual weather, e.g. snow or floods.
Q2 In order, the correct words are: cold; warm; stronger.
Q3 'Slow down and drive very carefully' and 'Avoid making unnecessary journeys' should be ticked.

Section 6 — Connecting to the World

Page 32

Q1 a) Town A
 b) 1. send each school a fax
    2. take a note to each school by car
    3. by post
Q2 a) Missing numbers are:
     from other businesses in Town A — 4
     from bookshops in Town B — 7
     total from City — 42
 b) 'Paper suppliers' and 'Food suppliers' should be ticked.

Page 33

Q1 The following things should be shaded:
 An e-mail can be sent very quickly;
 E-mails travel very quickly to far-away places;
 E-mails don't need stamps;
 E-mails don't have to be posted, sorted and sent by train, boat or plane;
 E-mails aren't untidy like some people's handwriting.
Q2 Write to a friend... — Letter
 Wish your uncle... — Card
 Tell someone what... — E-mail
Q3 a) MAP
 b) PHOTO
 c) BAR GRAPH

Page 34

Q1

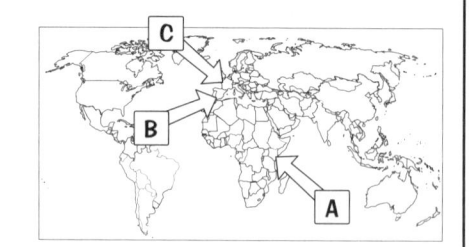

Q2 The airports are:
 Kenya — Nairobi
 France — Charles de Gaulle
 Spain — Malaga
Q3 In order, the missing words are: south; English; France; Malaga.

Page 35

Q1 travel agent; TV travel programme; websites; newspaper travel pages.
Q2 'Which airports in the UK have flights to Australia?'; 'How many hours will the journey take?' and 'Which places do we call at during the journey?' should be ticked.
Q3

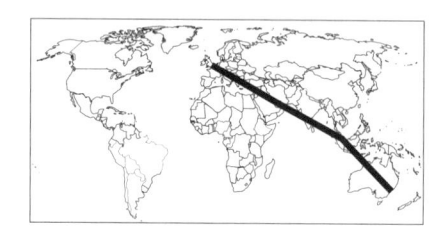

Section 7 — How Do We Spend Our Time?

Page 36

Q1 a) 3 hours
 b) 2 hours
 c) one hour
Q2 WORK — Doing jobs or being at school.
 LEISURE TIME — Free time, when you can do whatever you want.
 RECREATION — Doing something for fun in your spare time.
Q3 Work — doing sums; homework; history lesson.
 Leisure — watching TV; riding a bike; playing football.

Page 37

Q1 a) What do I want to find out?
 b) Who shall I ask?
 c) How many people shall I ask?
Q2 the 5 children on his table; all the children in his class.
Q3 Did you play football on Monday?
 Yes.
 How long did you play for?
 One hour.
 Where did you play football?
 In the park.

The Answers

Page 38

Q1 a) 5
     b) recreation ground
     c) Chetan and Gareth
     d) Gareth

Q2 On the map of Margam:
     a) The football symbol should be drawn on the Recreation Ground.
     b) The tennis symbol should be drawn on the Tennis Club.
     c) The judo symbol should be drawn on the college.
     d) The bike riding symbol should be drawn on the park.

Q3 The symbols in the key should match the symbols used on the map.

Page 39

Q1 a) Gareth
     b) 6 hours

Q2 Judo, football & tennis should be shaded.

Q3 a) Total time = 1 + 2 + 1 + 0.5 + 0.5
                       = 5.
     b) Average is 5 divided by 5
                       = 1 hour.

Page 40

Q1 a) dry
     b) windy
     c) snow
     d) rain

Q2 It rained all night so the football pitch was flooded.
It was very foggy so they closed the airport because the pilots couldn't see.
It was very windy so the builders couldn't work on our roof.

Q3 a) RAINING
     b) COLD WIND
     c) FOGGY

The Answers